Splish! Splash! WHOOSH! Ocean Life

Written by: Sonia Maria
Illustrated by: Selfi Sidabutar

Copyright © 2022 Sonia M Webster
All rights reserved under International and Pan-American Copyright Conventions.

No part of this publication may be reproduced, stored in a retrieval system or transmitted in any form or any means, electronic, mechanical, photocopying, recording or otherwise without the prior written permission of the copyright owner.

Contact us at roadreefpress@gmail.com

Library of Congress Control Number: 2022920622

Summary: Illustrations and rhyming text are used to introduce children to fish and animals in the ocean and share some of their unique habits. 1. Stories in rhyme; 2. Fish - Fiction; 3. Marine - Life Fiction.

ISBN Paperback 978-1-915695-09-3; Hardcover 978-1-915695-10-9; Electronic 978-1-915695-11-6

Author: Sonia Maria; Illustrator: Selfi Sidabutar; Illustrator: Winart
Printed and distributed in the United States.

For Jeremy and Sean
Love you lots!

Sun, sand and deep blue sea.
Eight quick legs just dashed by me!

Crab

My eight legs have knees that bend to the side,
that's why I scuttle sideways.
I have two big claws that I use to pinch
strangers on my grumpy days.
SNIP! SNIP! WHOOSH!

Starfish

I have tiny eyes on the tips of my arms
and many small legs beneath.
I move around to find my meal,
then take my time to eat.
Yum! Yum! Whoosh!

Hermit Crab

I borrow my home from shells I find.
Plain or fancy? I don't mind.
And when I'm too big for this cozy home,
I'll borrow the next, and away I will roam.
KNOCK! KNOCK! WHOOSH!

Turtle

I bury my eggs in the warm sand
on shore to hatch baby turtles,
a hundred or more.
They push out of the sand
and rush down to the sea.
They're tiny, adorable versions of me.

Pitter-patter! Whoosh!

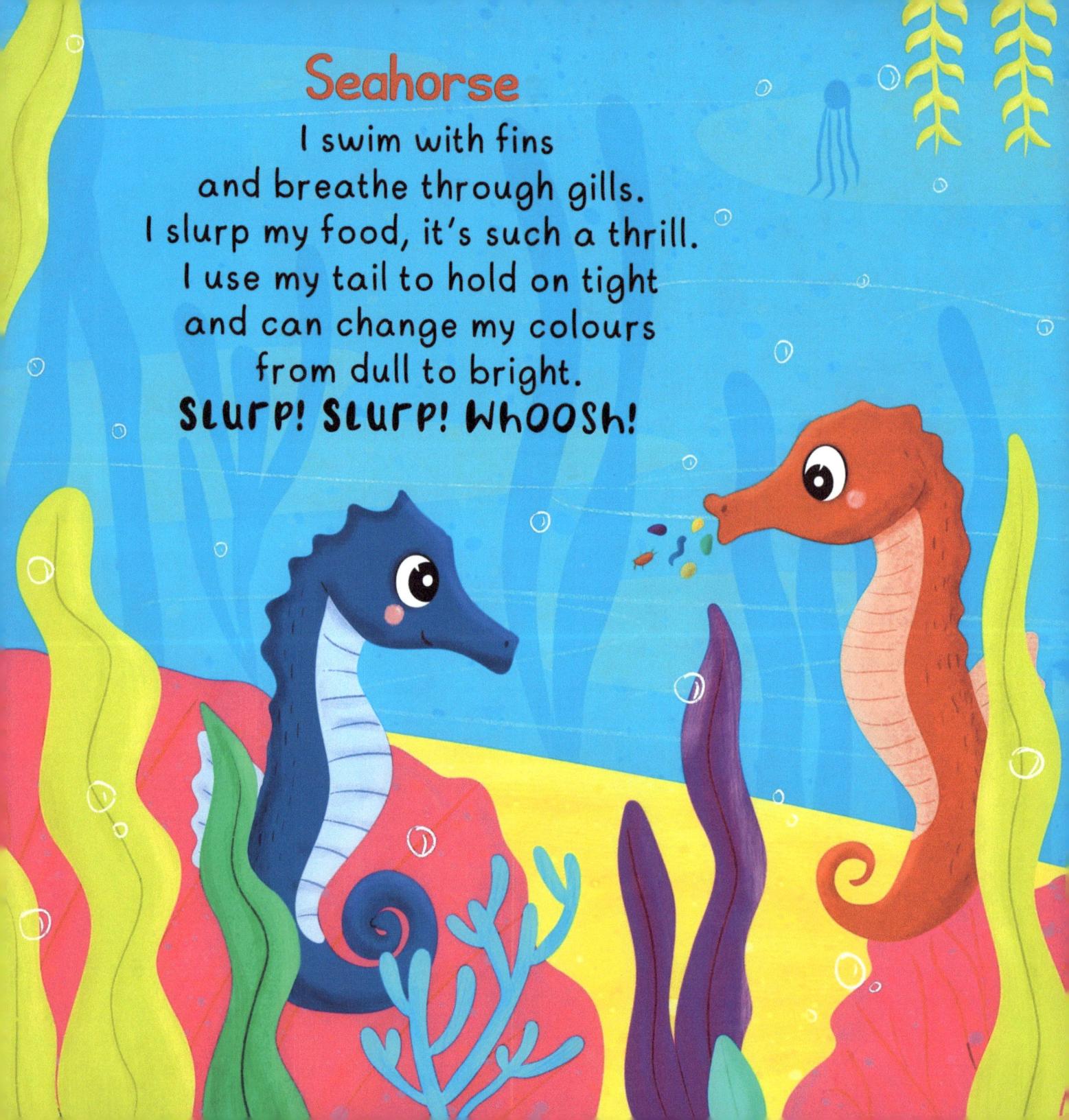

Seahorse

I swim with fins
and breathe through gills.
I slurp my food, it's such a thrill.
I use my tail to hold on tight
and can change my colours
from dull to bright.
Slurp! Slurp! Whoosh!

Octopus

I'm made mostly of muscles,
and so I am strong.
My eight arms have suckers
that can hold on for long.
I'm fast and flexible, smart as can be.
I'll squirt you with ink if you try to
catch me.
Squirt! Squirt! Whoosh!

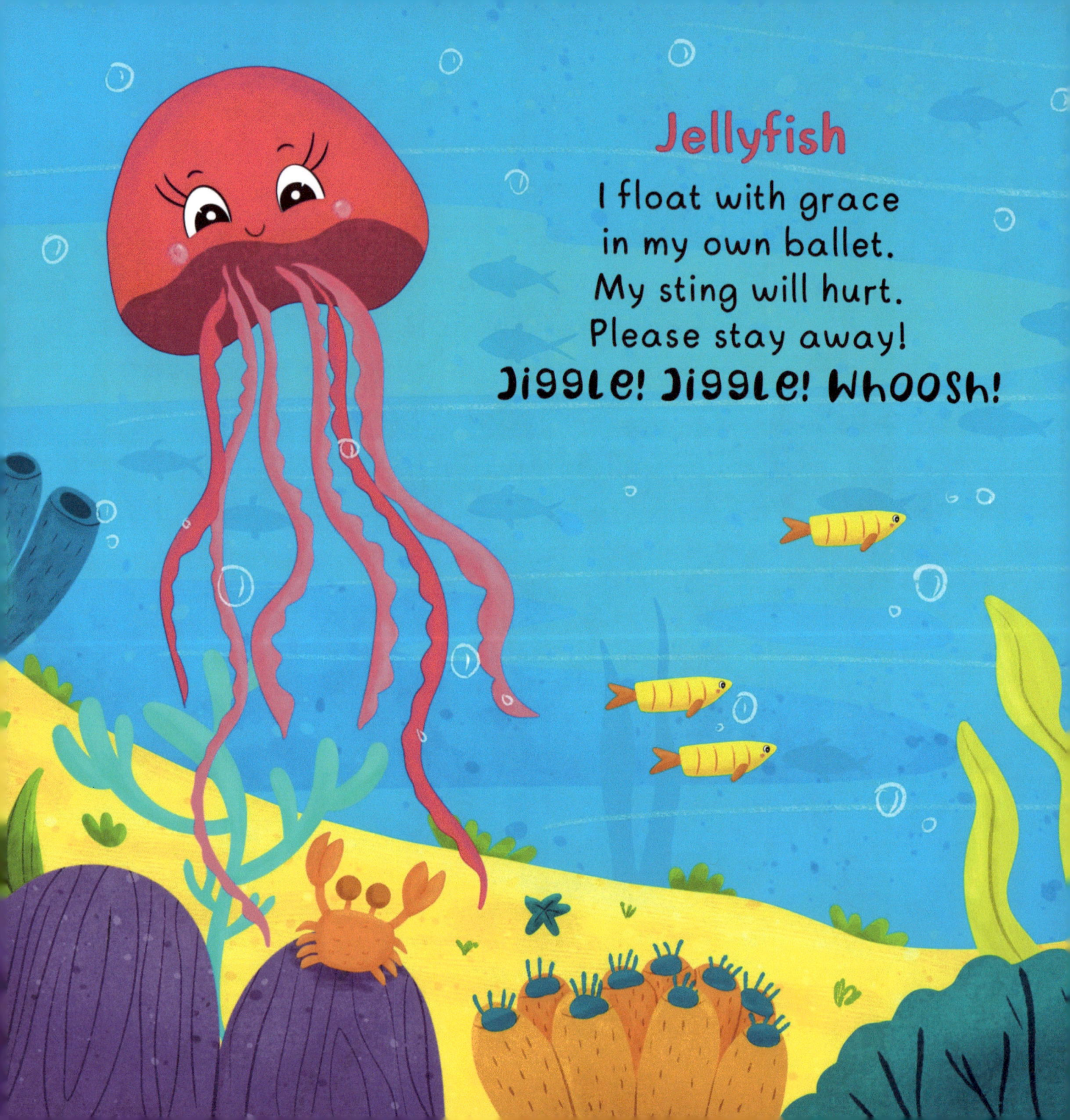

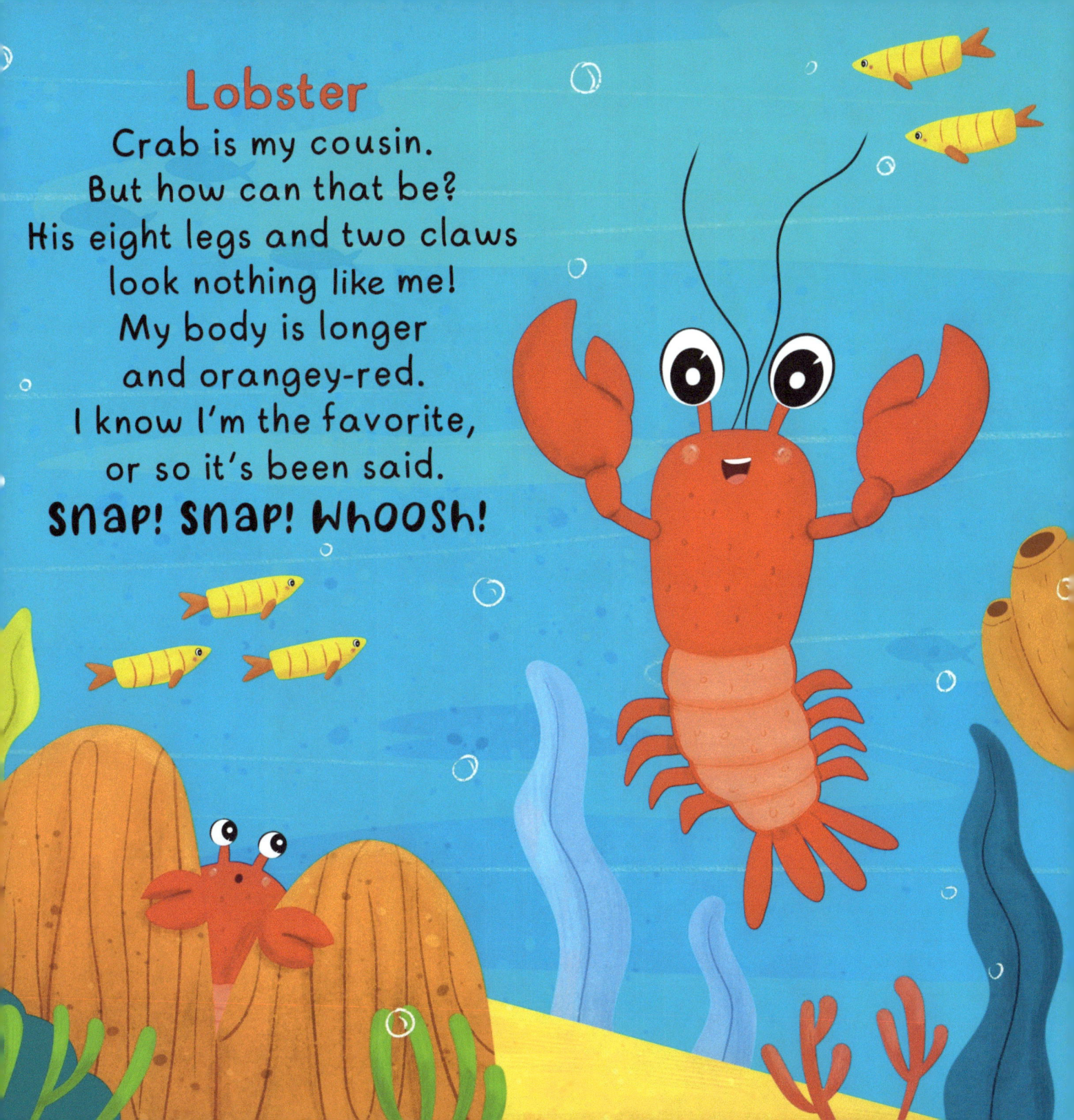

Lobster

Crab is my cousin.
But how can that be?
His eight legs and two claws
look nothing like me!
My body is longer
and orangey-red.
I know I'm the favorite,
or so it's been said.
SNAP! SNAP! WHOOSH!

Clownfish

I'm orange and white
all day and all night.
Some of my cousins are not.
Come visit again. I'm easy to find!
I hide in this very same spot.
Peek-a-boo! Whoosh!

School of Fish

We swim in a school with no teachers or class. It helps keep us safe as our numbers are vast.
RING! RING! WHOOSH!

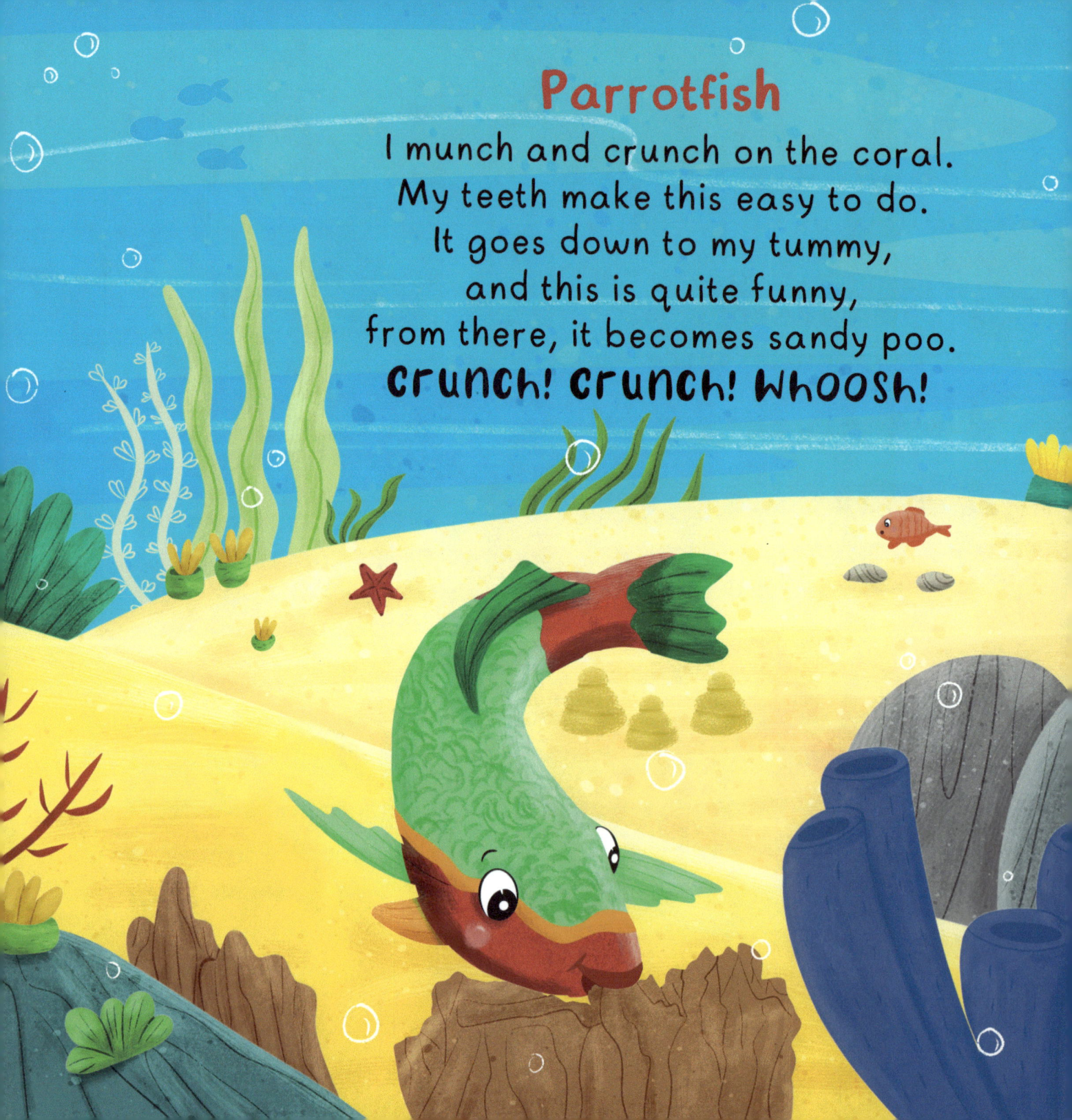

Parrotfish

I munch and crunch on the coral.
My teeth make this easy to do.
It goes down to my tummy,
and this is quite funny,
from there, it becomes sandy poo.
Crunch! Crunch! Whoosh!

Angelfish

The spike on my head is just splendid!
My colours are vibrant, it's true.
Some say that I'm striking.
That's much to my liking.
I think that I'm quite special too.
BLINK! BLINK! WHOOSH!

Flying Fish

I shoot out of the waves
when there's danger below
and glide through the air
in an impressive show.
BOOSH! BOOSH! WHOOSH!

Shark

I hunt for food.
I'm not afraid.
I'm fast and bold.
That's how I'm made.
CHOMP! CHOMP! WHOOSH!

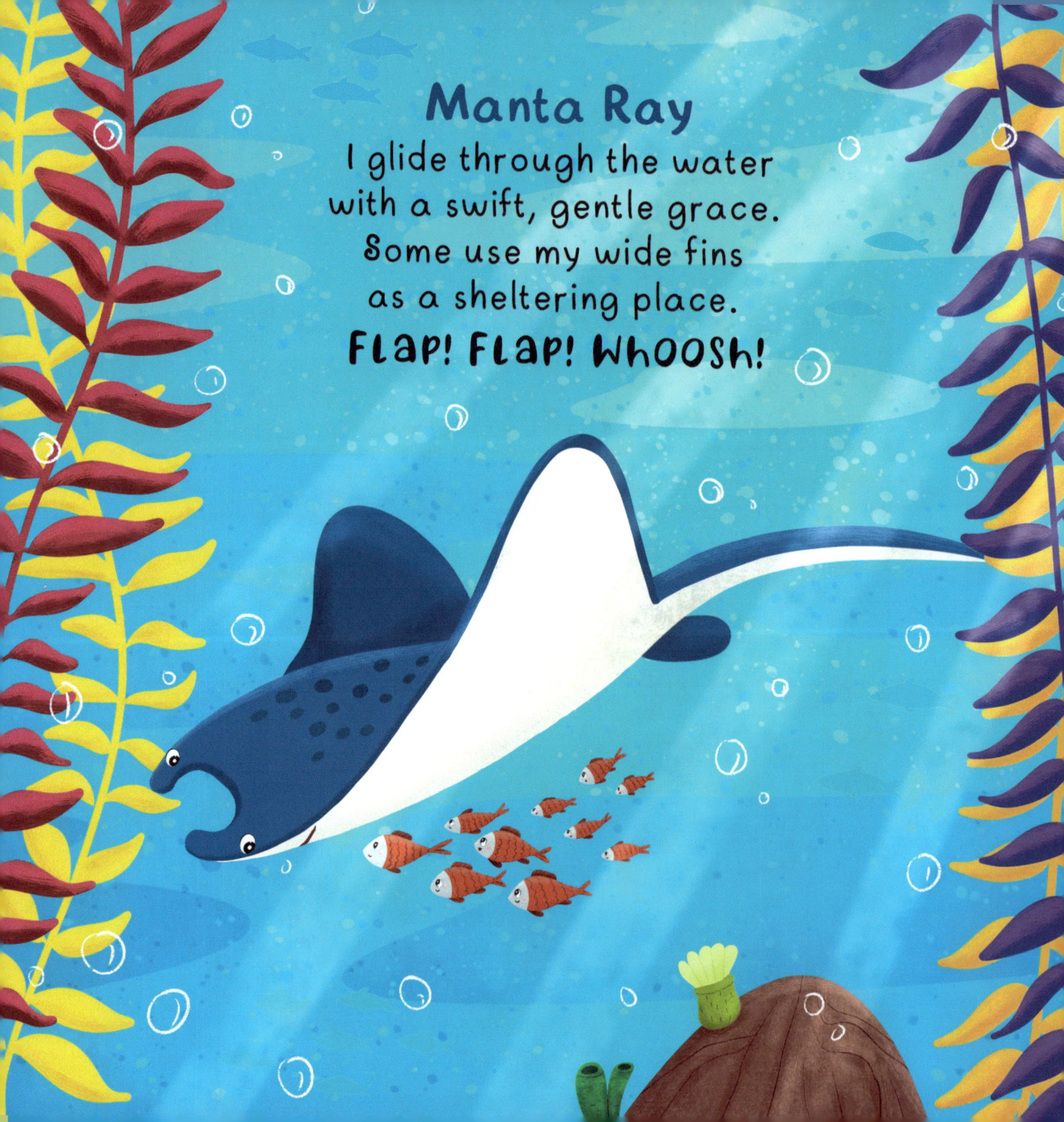

Manta Ray

I glide through the water
with a swift, gentle grace.
Some use my wide fins
as a sheltering place.
FLAP! FLAP! WHOOSH!

Dolphin

I like to play and chatter.
What else is there to do?
Come play with me, and you will see
that you will like it too.
Chatter! Chatter! Whoosh!

Blue Whale

The elephant is massive!
The largest on the land.
But I'm as big as thirty elephants.
Now isn't that just grand?
SWISH! SWISH! WHOOSH!

www.ingramcontent.com/pod-product-compliance
Lightning Source LLC
Chambersburg PA
CBHW041503220426
43661CB00016B/1239